RIVERS AND MOUNTAINS

By Joanna Brundle

KidHaven
PUBLISHING

TRANSFORMING EARTH'S GEOGRAPHY

Published in 2018 by
KidHaven Publishing, an Imprint of Greenhaven Publishing, LLC
353 3rd Avenue
Suite 255
New York, NY 10010

© 2018 Booklife Publishing
This edition is published by arrangement with Booklife Publishing.

Designer: Natalie Carr
Editor: Charlie Ogden

Photo credits: Abbreviations: l–left, r–right, b–bottom, t–top, c–center, m–middle.
Front Cover – orxy. 2 – Fesus Robert. 4 – Frontpage. 6 – Dchauy. 7t – Dmitry Burlakov. 7b – photomatz. 9t – Tawfik Dajani. 9b – phomphan. 10t – Menno Schaefer. 10b – defotoberg. 11t – dangdumrong. 11b – Egyptian Studio. 12r – Doug Meek. 13t – Tony Campbell. 13b – Patrizio Martorana. 14t – J.Schelkle. 14b – Dziewul. 15t – Vladimir Melnikov. 15b – IR Stone. 16t – Arthit Chamsat. 16b – wimpi. 17t – napocska. 17b – Mark Bridger. 18tr – Vixit. 18b – Shebeko. 20t – Pavel Svoboda Photography. 20b – By Horst_graben.jpg: U.S. Geological Survey derivative work: Gregors (talk) 11:17, 7 June 2011 (UTC) (Horst_graben.jpg) [Public domain], via Wikimedia Commons. 21 – Jose Gil. 22t – Ammit Jack. 22b – Wildnerdpix. 23t – Galyna Andrushko. 23b – Ursula Perreten. 24tr – Richard Whitcombe. 24m – CandyBox Images. 25b – Pavel Svoboda Photography. 26t – Top Photo Corporation. 26m – gorillaimages. 27t – Jacek_Kadaj. 27br –Tupungato. 28m – Mark Medcalf. 28bl – Vladimir Kogan Michael. 29t – tomtsya. 29b – Andrew Mayovskyy. 30t – Sakarin Sawasdinaka. 30m – S–F. Images are courtesy of Shutterstock.com, with thanks to Getty Images, Thinkstock Photo, and iStockphoto.

Cataloging-in-Publication Data

Names: Brundle, Joanna.
Title: Rivers and mountains / Joanna Brundle.
Description: New York : KidHaven Publishing, 2018. | Series: Transforming Earth's geography | Includes index.
Identifiers: ISBN 9781534524958 (pbk.) | 9781534524569 (library bound) | ISBN 9781534524965 (6 pack) | ISBN 9781534524613 (ebook)
Subjects: LCSH: Rivers–Juvenile literature. | Mountains–Juvenile literature.
Classification: LCC GB1203.8 B78 2018 | DDC 551.48'3–dc23

Printed in the United States of America

CPSIA compliance information: Batch #CW18KL: For further information contact Greenhaven Publishing LLC, New York, New York at 1-844-317-7404.

Please visit our website, www.greenhavenpublishing.com. For a free color catalog of all our high-quality books, call toll free 1-844-317-7404 or fax 1-844-317-7405.

RIVERS AND MOUNTAINS

CONTENTS

Words that appear like **this** can be found in the glossary on page 31.

WHAT ARE RIVERS?

Rivers are large streams of fresh water that flow across the land in a **channel**. Rivers flow downhill, typically into the ocean, but sometimes into large lakes. The bottom of the channel is called the riverbed. The source of a river is the place where it starts. The source may be a natural spring or a place where water collects. This water is generally either rainwater or water from melting snow and ice.

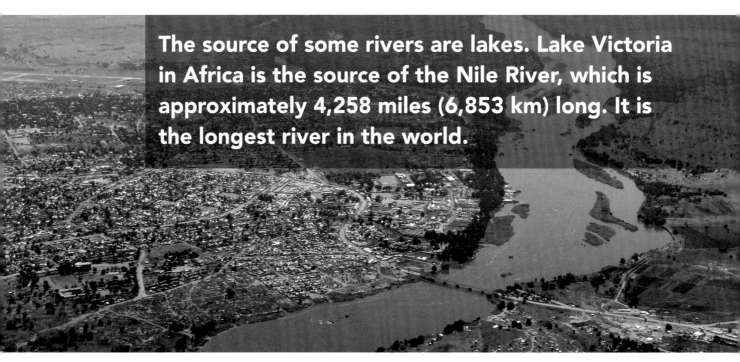

The source of some rivers are lakes. Lake Victoria in Africa is the source of the Nile River, which is approximately 4,258 miles (6,853 km) long. It is the longest river in the world.

Can you find out the name of the deepest river in the world? How deep is it? Use a map or globe to see where it flows. (The answer is on page 32.)

The collected water forms small channels called rills. As more water enters, bigger channels called gullies are formed. As the water trickles downhill, small streams join together to form a main stream, which widens into a river. Other small streams and rivers, called tributaries, may flow into the main river. The point where they meet is called the confluence.

THE WATER CYCLE

Rivers are an important part of the water cycle.

3) Water droplets fall as snow or rain.

2) Water vapor rises into the air, cools down, and condenses, forming clouds.

4) Streams and rivers carry the water back to the ocean.

1) The sun allows ocean water to evaporate.

A RIVER'S JOURNEY

The path that a river follows is called its course. To help us understand more about a river at each stage of its journey, **geographers** split each river's journey into upper, middle, and lower courses. The upper course is also called a young river. Think about how someone rushes around the playground, full of energy. Like this person, a young river moves quickly as it travels down steep slopes. The water in young rivers often looks white as it bubbles and froths.

The riverbed is worn away by rocks and gravel that are carried along by the energy of the young river. This process is called abrasion and it causes V-shaped **valleys** with steep sides to form.

As the river moves into its middle course, it is said to be middle-aged. As more tributaries flow into the main river, it becomes wider and deeper. The land it flows through becomes flatter, and the river moves more slowly. The shape of the valley that the river makes becomes broader and flatter. When it reaches its lower course, also known as old age, the river flows much more slowly and it snakes across the land in curves and loops called meanders. In its middle and lower courses, the river may be carrying large amounts of mud, soil, and silt—tiny pieces of sand and rock—that make the water look cloudy and muddy. The mouth of the river is the place where it flows into the ocean.

meander

river mouth

OXBOW LAKES AND FLOOD PLAINS

Rivers sometimes change direction. The flow of the water—which is known as the current—is faster on the outside of a bend than it is on the inside of a bend. This wears away the land on the outside of the bend, making the meander even bigger. On the inside of the bend, the slow-moving water leaves behind mud and other sediment, which build up to form new land. Over time, bends in the river move closer together and the river takes a shortcut between them. This leaves part of the river stranded and not touching the rest. We call this an oxbow lake.

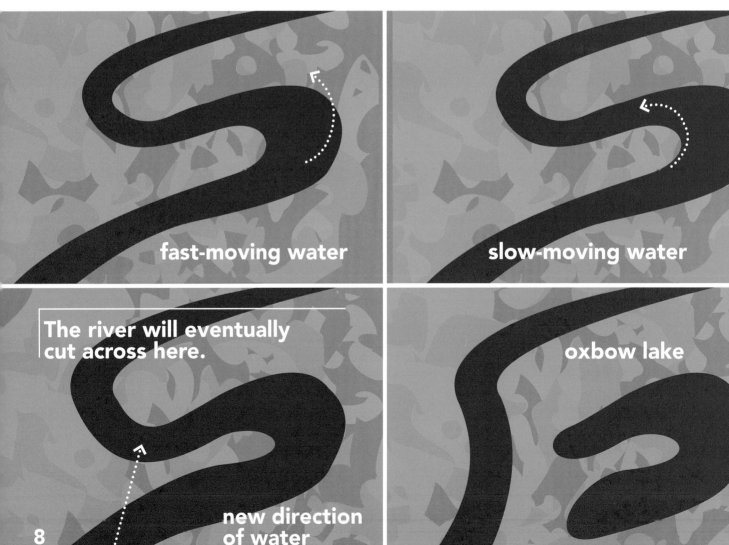

fast-moving water

slow-moving water

The river will eventually cut across here.

new direction of water

oxbow lake

During spells of heavy rain or periods when lots of snow melts, the water level of a river in its lower course may rise so much that it floods over its banks and onto the land, which is often known as a flood plain.

Sediment made up of mud, soil, and tiny particles of rock gets deposited on the flood plains, which makes the soil extremely **fertile**. Material that is deposited on a flood plain by an overflowing river is called alluvium.

Flooding can cause damage to homes and businesses, but it can also be a good thing. For thousands of years, farmers along the Nile River relied on its yearly floods to grow crops and bring water for their animals. They used to store the floodwaters in irrigation ditches for later use.

cattle grazing in Egypt

Farmland by the Mekong River in Vietnam is great for growing rice.

ESTUARIES AND DELTAS

As a river nears the sea, it widens out and may form a flat area called an estuary. The water in an estuary is known as brackish water—a mixture of fresh river water and salty sea water that washes into the river at **high tide**. The sediment carried in the slow-flowing water builds up to form mud flats, which attract wading birds, such as the bar-tailed godwits, that feed on creatures living in the mud. The mud smells like rotten eggs!

bar-tailed godwits

River levels in estuaries and the saltiness of the water are affected by the tides.

an estuary at low tide in Brittany, France

In the mouths of large rivers, the dropped sediment may form new, swampy islands of land called deltas. The delta of the Ganges River in the Bay of Bengal is called the Sundarbans or Brahmaputra Delta, and it is the largest delta in the world. It is home to rare Bengal tigers and lots of other wildlife.

Other rivers with large deltas include the Mississippi River and the Colorado River in the United States, the Orinoco River in Venezuela, and the Nile River in Egypt.

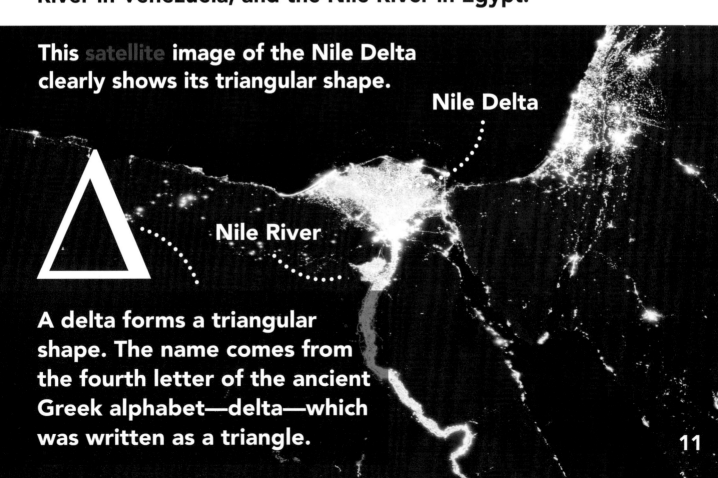

This satellite image of the Nile Delta clearly shows its triangular shape.

Nile Delta

Nile River

A delta forms a triangular shape. The name comes from the fourth letter of the ancient Greek alphabet—delta—which was written as a triangle.

11

CHANGING LANDSCAPES AND WATERWAYS

As they flow, rivers wear away and change the landscape. They carve out deep channels, called gorges or canyons, and create steep waterfalls.

Over millions of years, the Colorado River in the United States carved out the Grand Canyon. It is the longest, widest, and deepest canyon in the world.

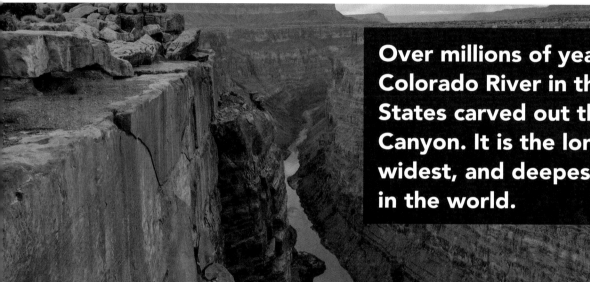

hard rock

soft rock

Soft rock is worn away here.

Waterfalls form in the upper course of a river where a layer of hard rock sits on top of layers of softer rock. The water wears away the softer rock more quickly than it wears away the harder rock, leaving an overhanging shelf or ledge. As the river pours over the ledge, it forms a waterfall. In time, the ledge collapses and the whole process starts again further **upstream**.

During a **drought**, the water level of a river may fall or the river may dry up completely. People and animals who rely on the river water for drinking, fishing, and farming purposes can face serious problems during droughts. Sometimes farmers contribute to the problem by taking too much water out of a river for irrigation. The Rio Grande, which has many large farms along its banks, is slowly drying up for this reason.

When a river dries up, many fish can become stranded and die.

Many rivers have been **polluted** by the actions of humans. Waste, such as tires, sewage, oil, and chemicals from factories, can find its way into rivers and destroy the **habitats** of wildlife. Modern farming methods can also lead to **fertilizers** and **pesticides** being washed into waterways. You can help by disposing of your garbage properly and by getting your school involved in a river care project.

Counting the number of fish is a reliable way to test a river's water quality.

USING AND CONTROLLING RIVERS

Rivers are useful! Wide, deep rivers enable boats and ships to travel inland, transporting people and **goods**. The Rhine River, which flows through Switzerland, Germany, and the Netherlands, is the busiest waterway in Europe. Timber and steel are some of the most important goods that are carried along it by boats and barges.

a barge traveling along the Rhine

Rivers generate hydroelectric power. The water in the river is controlled by a **dam** built across the river. The force of the water rushing through the dam turns turbines, generating electricity.

Rivers are fun too! People enjoy leisure activities in rivers such as swimming, fishing, and kayaking. Riverbanks are used by cyclists, dog walkers, bird watchers, and people enjoying picnics.

Always take care near rivers and follow all warning signs. Try to learn to swim, either at school or at your local swimming pool. Never swim in a river unless a responsible adult is with you and has checked that it is safe to do so.

Whitewater rafting is fun.

Humans have developed many ways to control the power of rivers. As well as providing electricity, dams can be used to prevent flooding. Reservoirs—the places behind dams where the water is collected and stored—provide a steady, reliable source of water for people and crops. Levees are high, man-made banks that are built to contain flooding rivers.

Floods can destroy farmlands and homes.

Completed in 1982, the 1,706-foot (520 m) wide Thames Barrier protects central London from flooding. Nine concrete barriers support ten steel gates. The gates lie on the riverbed but can be raised if there is a risk of flooding.

Thames Barrier

RIVER WILDLIFE AND PLANTS

Animals and plants **adapt** to suit their habitats, and river inhabitants are no exception. Oxygen is needed by all animals. Most fish have **gills** that enable them to absorb oxygen from the water. Other river creatures, such as leeches, absorb oxygen through their skin.

Fish have sleek, narrow bodies, which move easily through water. Archer fish hunt by firing jets of water at flying insects, which then fall into the water next to the hungry archer fish.

archer fish

Hippos have their eyes, ears, and nostrils on top of their heads, which enables them to see, hear, and breathe while they cool off in the water. They can also close their ears and nostrils when they go underwater.

hippos

Plants need sunlight to grow. Water blocks a large amount of sunlight from reaching underwater plants, so some have adapted to have leaves that reach above the surface or float on top of the river. Plants also absorb **nutrients** from the river water.

The leaves of these giant water lilies have many air pockets underneath them that help them to float.

Plants anchor themselves to the riverbed by attaching their roots to sediment or rocks. Some plants, such as tape grass, have long and thin leaves that easily bend with the water, stopping the plants from being uprooted.

Marginal plants, such as reeds, are plants that grow on the banks of rivers. Their roots spread out through the mud, and they can grow so thickly that new land is formed at the river's edge. Swans and other birds make their nests in these areas.

This swan is with its young. Young swans are called cygnets.

17

WHAT ARE MOUNTAINS?

Landforms are natural features of the earth's surface, and they include hills, valleys, and mountains. If you look around your local area, you will probably see that the earth's surface is not flat. The highest places on Earth are called mountains. They are found on all seven continents, in the middle of oceans, and even on other planets.

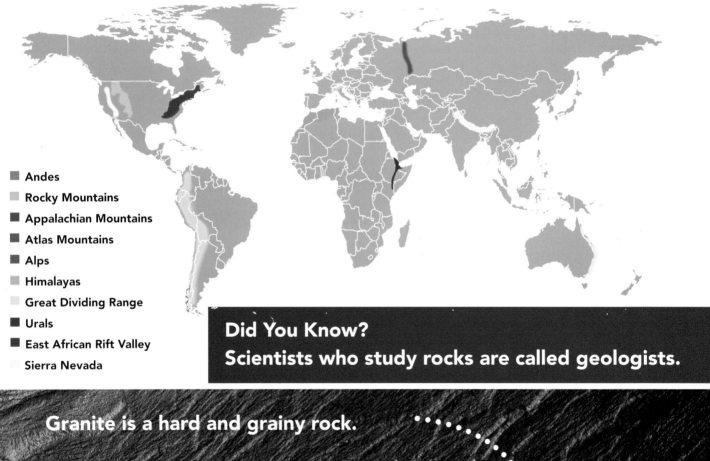

- Andes
- Rocky Mountains
- Appalachian Mountains
- Atlas Mountains
- Alps
- Himalayas
- Great Dividing Range
- Urals
- East African Rift Valley
- Sierra Nevada

Did You Know?
Scientists who study rocks are called geologists.

Granite is a hard and grainy rock.

Mountains cover approximately one-quarter of the total land on Earth, not including those parts covered by the ocean.

HOW DO MOUNTAINS FORM?

The top layer of the earth, called the crust, is similar to a giant jigsaw puzzle made up of huge slabs of rock. Although it feels solid under our feet, the giant slabs, called tectonic plates, are constantly moving on top of a layer of hot, molten rock underneath.

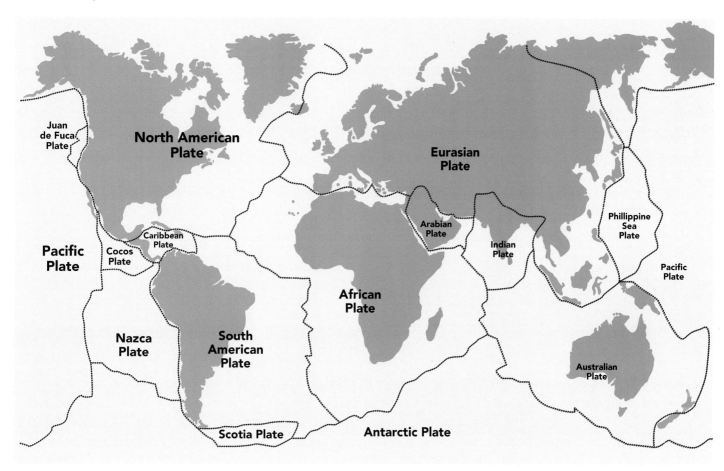

This map shows how the tectonic plates fit together.

When the plates collide or pull apart, they create huge amounts of pressure, and rock may be forced upward, forming mountains. The plates move slowly, at about the same rate as your fingernails grow, and it can take millions of years for mountains to form.

The Himalayas in Asia were formed by the Indian Plate pushing against the Eurasian Plate. They are still growing by about 2.4 inches (6 cm) a year as the plates continue to push together. They are considered to be quite young mountains, as they only began to form about 600,000 years ago!

DIFFERENT TYPES OF MOUNTAINS

The movement of the earth's tectonic plates produces three main types of mountains: fold mountains, block mountains, and dome mountains. To understand how fold mountains form, lay out a towel or another piece of cloth in front of you. Push the edges of the towel or cloth together with two hands. Your hands are acting like tectonic plates. Folds appear, just like mountains being pushed up, as the tectonic plates grind together.

Block mountains are formed when cracks in the earth's crust, known as faults, force blocks of hard rock to either push up and form a mountain or collapse down to form a valley with block mountains on either side. The peaks of block mountains, such as those of the Sierra Nevada in the United States, are flatter than those of fold mountains.

The Andes in South America are fold mountains. Fold mountains are generally made out of softer, sedimentary rock, such as sandstone, and often have jagged peaks. Other examples of fold mountains include the Rocky Mountains and the Urals.

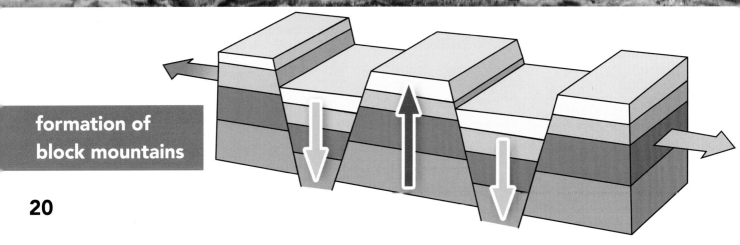

formation of block mountains

The hot, molten rock under the earth's crust is called magma. Dome mountains are formed when vast amounts of magma force the earth's crust upward without breaking through it. The magma pushes up the layers of rock that are on top of it to form a mountain. In cases where the magma does break through the earth's crust, it is called an eruption. Dome mountains have a distinctive domed shape that looks like the top half of a tennis ball.

Half Dome in Yosemite National Park

Did you Know? – The longest mountain range in the world lies under the sea! It is called the Mid-ocean Ridge and runs through every ocean on the planet. It is 40,389 miles (65,000 km) long.

VOLCANOES

Volcanoes are places where magma from deep within our planet explodes through the earth's crust. The molten rock, which is known as lava once it reaches the surface, then cools and hardens to form new rock. This new rock then builds up over time to form a mountain. Most volcanoes form along plate boundaries, where tectonic plates come together.

The shape of volcanic mountains depends on the type of material that they erupt. The highest volcanic mountains are stratovolcanoes and shield volcanoes. Stratovolcanoes are tall, pointed cones that are made up of layers of cooled, thick lava and ash. Shield volcanoes form when runny lava spreads out over a wide area, building a gently sloping mountain.

Cotopaxi is an active stratovolcano in the Ecuadorian Andes.

Mauna Loa, a shield volcano in Hawaii, is the world's largest active volcano.

CHANGING MOUNTAINS: WEATHERING AND EROSION

The size and shape of a mountain changes constantly due to weathering and erosion. Weathering is a process in which rocks are broken down into smaller pieces by the action of the weather. For example, water that freezes in the gaps between rocks expands as it freezes, cracking the rocks apart. Erosion is the gradual wearing away that occurs due to ice, water, or wind.

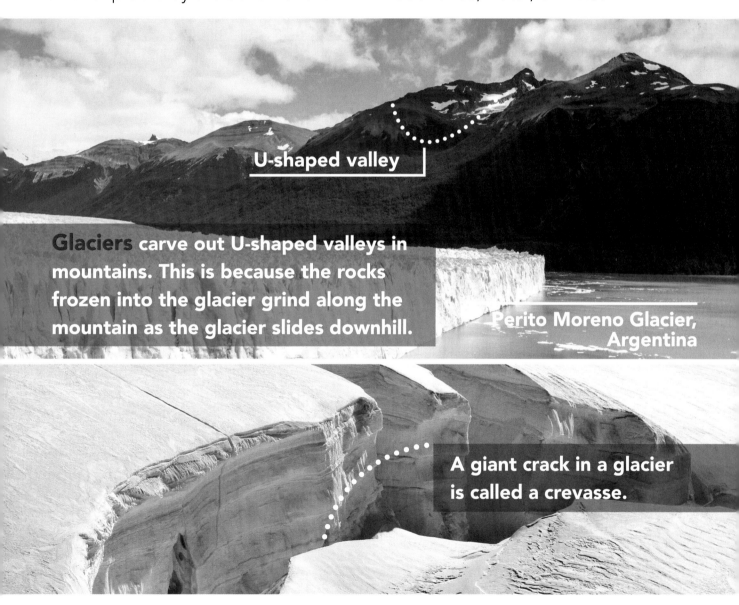

U-shaped valley

Glaciers carve out U-shaped valleys in mountains. This is because the rocks frozen into the glacier grind along the mountain as the glacier slides downhill.

Perito Moreno Glacier, Argentina

A giant crack in a glacier is called a crevasse.

Small, loose rocks also fall down the mountain, pulled by the force of **gravity**. They break off more rocks as they fall. Heaps of these broken rocks, called scree, collect at the base of mountain slopes.

MOUNTAIN WEATHER

The average weather of an area, relating to things such as its rainfall and temperature, is known as its climate. A climate zone is an area that has a climate that is different from that of its neighboring areas. The great height of mountains means that a single mountain typically has several different zones, each with its own climate. At the highest zone, there is generally only ice and snow, and it is extremely cold and windy.

Mountain rescue teams, sometimes helped by specially trained dogs, rescue people who are stuck on the sides of mountains. Rescue helicopters are used when people need to be rescued from more remote areas.

The snowline is the level above which a mountain is permanently covered in snow, even in the summer. Further down, in the middle and lower zones, the climate is warm enough for people, plants, and animals to survive, at least for some of the year. Mountain weather can change quickly. Thick clouds and fierce storms can appear suddenly. Blizzards can whip the snow into snowdrifts, while melting snow can trigger an avalanche.

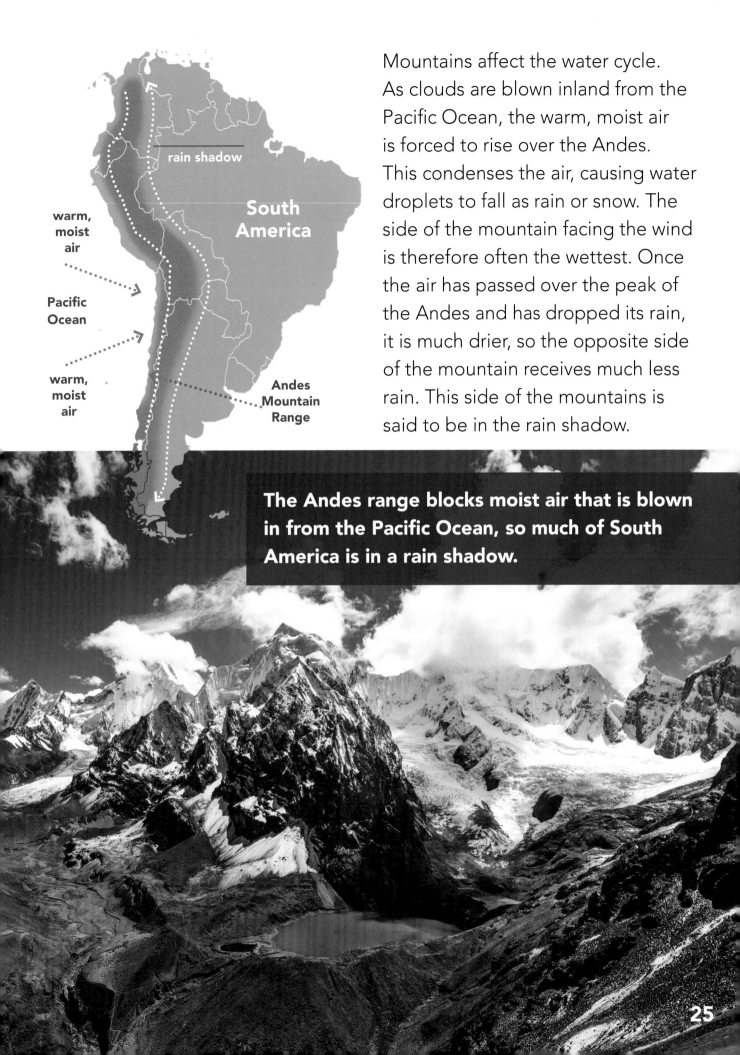

Mountains affect the water cycle. As clouds are blown inland from the Pacific Ocean, the warm, moist air is forced to rise over the Andes. This condenses the air, causing water droplets to fall as rain or snow. The side of the mountain facing the wind is therefore often the wettest. Once the air has passed over the peak of the Andes and has dropped its rain, it is much drier, so the opposite side of the mountain receives much less rain. This side of the mountains is said to be in the rain shadow.

rain shadow

South America

warm, moist air

Pacific Ocean

warm, moist air

Andes Mountain Range

The Andes range blocks moist air that is blown in from the Pacific Ocean, so much of South America is in a rain shadow.

LIVING IN THE MOUNTAINS

Many mountain people survive by farming in the lower, warmer zones near the bottom of the mountain. They cut steps, called terraces, into the mountain so that they have flat land on which to grow their crops. Terraces also help to stop the soil from being washed away by heavy rain.

terraced farm

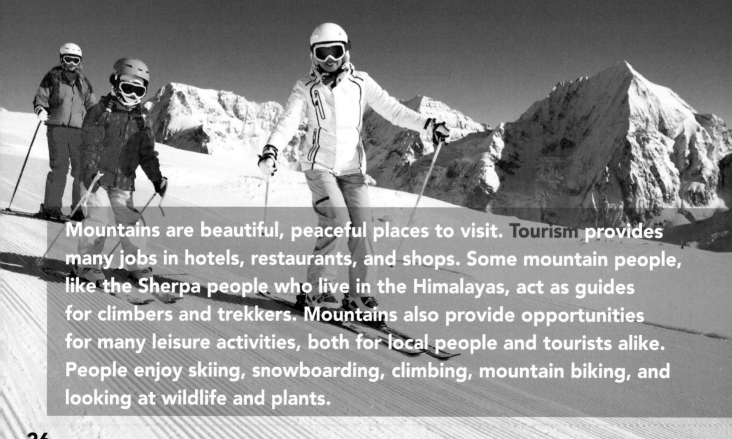

Mountains are beautiful, peaceful places to visit. Tourism provides many jobs in hotels, restaurants, and shops. Some mountain people, like the Sherpa people who live in the Himalayas, act as guides for climbers and trekkers. Mountains also provide opportunities for many leisure activities, both for local people and tourists alike. People enjoy skiing, snowboarding, climbing, mountain biking, and looking at wildlife and plants.

Some mountain people keep animals, using every part of the animal to help them survive. In the Andes, people keep alpacas—animals that are similar to llamas—that provide them with meat and milk. Skins and wool from the animals are used to make clothes, blankets, and ropes. Even the dung is used—it is burnt as fuel!

Children in Peru, dressed in traditional clothes, are shown here with their alpacas.

Every living thing needs to breathe oxygen, which is a gas that can be found in air, in order to stay alive. The higher up a mountain you go, the less oxygen the air contains, meaning that it becomes harder to breathe. The air is said to be "thin," and it causes some people to feel unwell from a condition known as altitude sickness. People living high up in the mountains are thought to have bigger lungs and hearts that help them to cope with this problem.

Mountain people have to deal with harsh conditions. Mountain homes are built with steep, sloping roofs, so that snow and ice slide off.

MOUNTAIN WILDLIFE AND PLANTS

Mountain goats have thick, woolly coats that protect them from wind and snow. They are able to jump between rocks and balance on narrow mountain ridges thanks to their well-adapted hooves. Their hooves split into two toes, and they have a soft pad to give them a better grip.

Mountain goats have soft, flexible hooves, making it easy for them to keep their grip as they jump from rock to rock.

Mountains are windy places. Golden eagles have a huge wingspan, which helps them to soar through the air as they hunt for food. Their sharp eyes enable them to spot **prey**, which they grasp in their strong, curved claws, called talons.

Different plants grow in each of the climate zones on a mountain. Forests of **deciduous trees** cover the lower slopes. Higher up, hardy, **coniferous trees** grow, such as spruce and pine trees. Their tough bark protects them from the wind and cold, and their cone shape helps snow to slide off without breaking any branches.

Shown here are coniferous trees on a mountain.

Each spring, plants grow higher up the mountain than any of the trees do. Known as alpine plants, they grow close to the ground. They have short stems and strong roots that help to stop them from being blown away. Many are protected from the cold by tiny hairs on their stems and leaves.

If you go exploring in the mountains, be sure to stay safe! Wear suitable clothes and footwear and carry food, water, a phone, and first aid items. Always check the weather forecast and walk in a group.

SURPRISING MOUNTAINS

Mount Fuji in Japan is a sacred place for followers of the Buddhist and Shinto religions. Every summer, thousands of people climb the mountain.

Mount Fuji

The ancient Greeks believed that 12 gods, including the leader of the gods, Zeus, lived on Mount Olympus.

The Olympic Games were originally held to honor Zeus and are named after Mount Olympus.

Some seamounts, which are mountains that formed under the sea, are taller from top to bottom than Mount Everest. Mount Everest goes higher into the sky because these seamounts start deep underwater. The two highest seamounts, Mauna Loa and Mauna Kea, are over 33,464 feet (10,200 m) tall and form part of the island of Hawaii, where they rise above the surface of the ocean.

The highest known mountain in the solar system is on Mars, and it is called Olympus Mons. It is around 15.5 miles (25 km) high, which is three times higher than Mount Everest.

GLOSSARY

adapt	to change over time to suit different conditions
avalanche	a large, often dangerous, mass of snow and rocks that rushes down a mountain
blizzard	a snowstorm
channel	a groove or dip in the ground where water flows
condense	to change from a gas (water vapor) into a liquid (water)
coniferous tree	a tree that produces cones and has needle-shaped leaves that stay green all year round
dam	a man-made structure built across a river to control the water
deciduous tree	a tree with large leaves that fall off in the autumn
drought	a period of dry weather that causes water shortages
evaporate	to turn from a liquid into a gas, typically because of heat
fertile	able to grow strong, healthy crops
fertilizer	a substance added to crops to help them to grow
geographer	a scientist who studies the earth's surface and populations
gill	the body part of fish that enables them to take in oxygen from the water
glacier	a large mass of ice that moves slowly
good	a useful item that is bought and sold
gravity	the force that pulls all objects towards the center of the earth
habitat	a place where plants or animals live
high tide	when the sea's tide is all the way in
irrigation	adding water to crops to help them to grow
low tide	when the sea's tide is all the way out
nutrient	a substance needed by animals and plants in order to grow
pesticide	a chemical used to kill animals and insects that damage crops
pollute	to contaminate with harmful or poisonous substances
prey	a creature that is hunted by another animal for food
satellite	a machine that orbits Earth, taking photographs and collecting information
tourism	traveling to places for leisure activities and sightseeing
upstream	against the flow of the current, toward the source of a river
valley	a low-lying area of land between hills or mountains, generally with a stream or river flowing through it
water vapor	water in the form of a gas

INDEX

**Page 4 Answer:
Congo River in
Africa. It is over
721 feet (220 m)
deep in places.**